IMAGES
of America

MURRIETA

FOUNTAIN HOUSE HOTEL, C. 1910. Katie Sleeper and her niece Hale Sykes stand in front of the Fountain House Hotel, the hub of activity in Murrieta, across Clay Avenue from the Murrieta Train Depot.

ON THE COVER: This is the last annual Fourth of July Picnic on B Street in 1914. Before the picnic, ladies fried chicken and packed bread, tableware, and linens into wicker baskets. The decorating committee hung red, white, and blue bunting. Children waved flags, ran sack and foot races, and played badminton games. Everyone had a good time until a spectator named Mr. Carrillo leaned too far forward during a horse race and was killed. That was the end of the Fourth of July Picnics. Some of the juniper trees in this photograph are still standing on B Street, which was called Lovers Lane, east of Washington Avenue.

IMAGES

of America

MURRIETA

Marvin Curran, Loretta Barnett,
and Rebecca Farnbach

ARCADIA
PUBLISHING

Published by Arcadia Publishing
Charleston, South Carolina

Library of Congress Catalog Card Number: 2006926310

For all general information contact Arcadia Publishing at:
Telephone 843-853-2070
Fax 843-853-0044
E-mail sales@arcadiapublishing.com
For customer service and orders:
Toll-Free 1-888-313-2665

Visit us on the Internet at www.arcadiapublishing.com

We dedicate this book to E. Hale Curran, who left a legacy by compiling a photographic history of Murrieta. This forward-thinking woman captured some of the photographs used in this book with her own camera and collected others to depict life during times past in Murrieta.

CONTENTS

ACKNOWLEDGMENTS

The photographs in this book are from E. Hale Curran's extensive collection, except for those noted otherwise. While she was alive, Hale freely shared her photographs and stories about Murrieta with anyone who asked. Her children, Marvin Curran and Kay Hudson, now open Hale's photograph albums to the community, and we authors attempt to retell the stories of the photographs.

We want to acknowledge the work of three other women for their contributions to preserving the stories of the history of Murrieta. We appreciate the work of the late Octavia Curran who spent hours interviewing her mother-in-law, Hale, and then produced reliable transcriptions. We also want to acknowledge Mary Alice Rail Boyce for her comprehensive book *Murrieta, Old Town, New Town* and Arlean Garrison's wonderful book *My Children's Home*. We referenced these books and other materials for the information in our captions.

We thank Alta Curran for her assistance during the compilation of the book. We thank our proofreaders Malcolm Barnett, Darell Farnbach, Dick Fox, and Bill Harker for checking our work before it went to press, and we thank Steven Allen for scanning the photographs.

If you wonder why certain people or events aren't featured in this book, it is because we used photographs and information at hand. If you have photographs or information you would like to share with community historians, please contact the Murrieta Library Heritage Room.

HALE WITH CAMERA, SEPTEMBER 5, 1917. Emma Hale Sykes was born in 1900 in a small house at First and A Streets. When her mother died a few days after giving life to Hale, Katie Sleeper, an aunt, raised her. She refused to be called Emma. Hale owned the box camera from the time she was a young girl and used it into the 1940s, when she could no longer find film for it. Growing up in Katie Sleeper's hotel across the street from the Murrieta Railroad Depot, she viewed the world from behind the shutter, documenting life as she saw it.

INTRODUCTION

The first thing that needs to be known about the town of Murrieta is that it was named after Juan Murrieta, an investor from Spain, not the infamous bandit Joaquin Murieta. Juan Murrieta left his home in Santurce, Spain, at the age of 17, and with two brothers, he sailed to the Americas. Juan and his brother Ezequiel bought land and cattle in California. They owned property in San Simeon, San Luis Obispo, and Merced. They later sold their cattle to buy sheep, because wool became a valued commodity after the cotton fields of the South were destroyed during the Civil War. An 1872 drought in Central California prompted Juan and Ezequiel Murrieta to look for greener pastures for their sheep, and they found the lush Temecula Valley.

In 1873, the Murrieta brothers, with partner Domingo Pujol and lawyer Francisco Sanjurjo, bought the 52,000 acres of the Temecula and Pauba Ranchos from Jacob Snyder and his associates. After just three years, the partnership dissolved and land was divided, probably according to the size of each investment. Pujol received almost 37,000 acres, their accountant and manager Jose Gonzalez received 60 acres, and Juan and Ezequiel Murrieta received 15,000 acres in the northern portion of the holdings, which included mineral hot springs. Pujol leased out his land and returned to Spain, where he died in 1881. His widow sold his properties to the Pauba Land and Water Company.

In 1882, Ezequiel Murrieta had returned to Spain when Juan Murrieta sold Ezequiel's holdings to the California Southern Railroad. In 1884, Juan sold all but 1,000 acres around his home to the Temecula Land and Water Company and moved his growing family from the ranch to Los Angeles. The Temecula Land and Water Company laid out plots for the new town of Murrietaville.

While Murrieta invested his tidy fortune in real estate in Los Angeles, the town of Murrieta grew. Families arrived by train to escape ravishing Midwestern winters and to invest sweat equity in sunny Southern California. Farms and businesses sprang up along the railway, and the little town became a destination for travelers seeking entertainment and healing of the hot springs where Juan Murrieta once washed his sheep.

Parker Dear and his wife, Elena Couts Dear, brought culture to the area when they moved onto the neighboring Santa Rosa Rancho in the 1880s. Parker, the son of the Englishman John Dear who invested in the Santa Rosa Rancho, built the beautiful Queen Anne–style home on the plateau. They hosted annual May Day picnics for residents of Murrieta.

Stories of a few of Murrieta's significant people, places, and buildings are found on the pages of this book. The little town grew, and by the late 1940s, a volunteer fire department was formed. Before the city of Murrieta incorporated in 1991, town business was conducted at the fire station. At the time of this publication, the city of Murrieta has a growing population of 93,000 and covers 44 square miles. The city has a hospital, a bible college, and 16 public schools, with three more planned.

Back to the confusion of the Murrieta name, it didn't stop with the bandit Murieta and the landowner and sheepherder Murrieta. Shortly after the promotion of Murrietaville by developers, the last syllable was dropped, and in 1885, when the application was written for a Murrieta post office, the person completing it spelled it "Murrietta." It wasn't until 1924 that the spelling was corrected to honor the two brothers who once owned the land, but the confusion didn't end. When fire chief Marvin Curran went to Ocala, Florida, to pick up Murrieta's new fire engine in

1990, "Marrietta" was painted on the door. Today the city enjoys a uniform spelling by all but troubled spellers.

Unlike the infamous criminal Joaquin Murieta, the founder of the city went on to be a lawman who served as a deputy sheriff in Los Angeles and puttered with horticulture until he died as an old man.

The authors are pleased to present this book to people who are interested in the history of Murrieta. And it is our belief that Hale Curran would be pleased that her photographs were put into this book and that the proceeds from the sale of the book are going toward building the Heritage Room of the Murrieta Public Library.

One

EARLY DAYS
OF MURRIETA

JUAN MURRIETA, C. 1885. When Juan and Ezequiel Murrieta arrived in the Temecula Valley with their sheep, the open grasslands provided welcome relief from the drought of Central California. It took three trips to drive their 100,000 sheep into the valley that flowed with artesian wells. (Photograph courtesy of Juan Murrieta's grandson, Dr. Thomas Murrieta.)

JUAN MURRIETA AT AGE 30, 1876. The Murrietas and their partners bought the 52,000 acres of the Pauba and Temecula Ranchos for a $1 an acre and reintroduced sheep to the area where sheep from the San Luis Rey Mission had grazed until the mission was closed in the 1830s. When bands of Mexican marauders came through the region in those early days, threatening ranchers with their machetes, Murrieta, knowing they wanted food, would butcher a sheep and hang the carcass far from his ranch house to keep his household safe.

ADELE GOLSH MURRIETA, C. 1876. When Juan met Adele, she lived with her family in Pala, far from her birthplace in Vienna, Austria. Adele's father, a cousin to both Austrian emperor Franz Joseph and Mexican emperor Maximilian, was exiled from Austria after the Austro-Prussian War. He sought asylum in Mexico, but when the family arrived in Mexico, Benito Juarez had killed Maximilian by firing squad. The displaced family eventually settled in the Pala Valley.

THE MURRIETA ADOBE, 1886. Pictured, from the left to right, are Ami Golsh, Juan Murrieta with son Henry, Adele Golsh Murrieta with daughter Lita, Mrs. Worthington and daughter Henrietta, Mr. Butcher with a dog, and an unidentified priest. The adobe was demolished after destruction during an earthquake on Christmas Day in 1899. The property was purchased in 1904 by Eli Barnett and was later Leo Roripaugh's ranch. (Photograph courtesy of Juan Murrieta's granddaughter Ann Smith, daughter of Lita.)

HUTCHINSON AND BROWN DAIRY, C. 1890. During the 1880s and 1890s, the Hutchinsons and Browns leased the Murrieta home and land, seen above, across modern day Jefferson Avenue from the Federal Express office. Pictured, from the left to right, are Bessie Gonzalez with her bicycle, Albert Hutchinson, Viola Hutchinson, Sara Hutchinson, and Johnny Rooney on a horse. The horseman in the background is not identified.

THE MURRIETA HOME IN LOS ANGELES, C. 1890. The family moved to this home in the North Broadway area of Los Angeles. Pictured here, from left to right, are A. J. "Jack" Murrieta, Henry Murrieta, Juan Murrieta holding Adela "Lita" Murrieta, Adele Golsh Murrieta, Arthur Golsh Jr., Arthur Golsh Sr., and Michael Golsh. (Photograph courtesy of Dr. Thomas Murrieta, son of A. J. Murrieta.)

MURRIETA FAMILY IN HOME ON COLLEGE STREET, C. 1900. The former sheepherder did well for himself, as evidenced by the plush furnishings of his home. A Luiseno pattern basket on the floor near the door is a memento from the Temecula Valley. (Photograph courtesy of Dr. Thomas Murrieta.)

MURRIETAS ON COLLEGE STREET PORCH, C. 1895. Juan was an avid horticulturist. He and Adele frequently showed plumerias and climbing lilies in Los Angeles flower exhibits. The California Avocado Growers Association credited him as being one of the introducers and earliest growers of avocados in California. Murrieta was acquainted with a Señor Fuentes, the Wells Fargo agent in Atlixco, Mexico, who sent Murrieta some avocado seeds. Dr. Tom Murrieta recalls a two-story-tall avocado tree at his *abuelo's* home in Los Angeles that had several of his grandfather's hybrid varieties of avocados growing on it, including the Colorado, Murrieta Green, and the Two-Pound Green. At one time, the Murrietas had about 20 avocado trees at their College Street residence. Juan enjoyed growing tropical and subtropical fruits, too. He planted several fruit trees at their adobe in Temecula Valley before moving to Los Angeles. (Photograph courtesy of Ann Smith.)

JUAN MURRIETA WITH LOS ANGELES COUNTY SHERIFF'S DEPARTMENT, 1929. After Murrieta sold his land in the Temecula Valley, he moved to Los Angeles and became the first deputy sheriff in 1886. Murrieta served the department for 39 years. In this photograph, Murrieta is holding the No. 1 badge awarded him by the sheriff's department, which is still owned by the family. (Photograph courtesy of Ann Smith.)

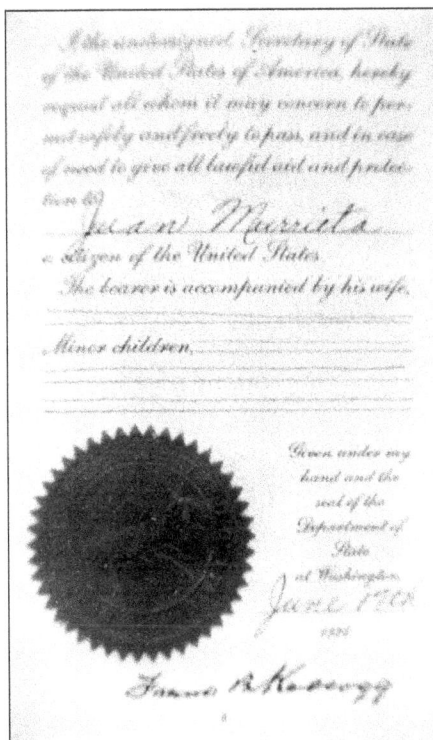

JUAN MURRIETA'S PASSPORT. Murrieta came to California in 1864 from the Basque Region of Bilbao, Spain, and became a United States citizen in 1875. His wife, Adele, preceded in him death by 15 years, and he spent his waning years in the Van Nuys home of his daughter Lita. He passed away in 1936, at the age of 92 years, and is buried in Calvary Cemetery in Los Angeles. (Photograph is courtesy of Dr. Thomas Murrieta.)

15

EARLIEST KNOWN PICTURE OF MURRIETA, C. 1900. The view, looking southeast from the foothills of the Santa Rosa Mountains near the end of Juniper Street, shows the hills called the hogbacks. The Murrieta Hot Springs are near the base of the largest hogback mountain. The trees are at Murrieta Creek, the school is to the far left, and the Hutchinsons' house is to the far right. The Fountain House Hotel is in the middle of the photograph. The streets were laid out in a grid pattern, with avenues named after presidents running north to south and streets with names of trees crossing them, starting alphabetically with Apricot and Banana at the south end of town and ending with Nutmeg. Streets named for letters of the alphabet are interspersed between those named for trees. Winchester Road was originally named Banana Street.

Murrieta Depot Agent Miller and Daughter Evelyn, January 1898. The depot signs indicate the baggage room and waiting room; another identifies the depot as a Wells Fargo Express Station. Willard Miller served as postmaster and depot agent, assisted by his daughter Evelyn. Miller only had one arm and would pull a small wagon to carry things to the train. Miller Canyon, at the end of Juniper Street, was named for the Miller family.

RAILROAD CONSTRUCTION, 1882. The coming of the rail line meant less isolation for the determined pioneers of the valley. It brought more availability of goods and ease of getting produce to the market. Businesses sprang up in the new town of Murrieta, and newcomers arrived by train. The photograph shows a very old steam shovel.

BUILDING THE ATCHISON, TOPEKA AND SANTA FE RAILROAD THROUGH RIVERSIDE. The work crews were largely Mexican and Chinese. Much of their work was done by hand with pick and shovel. They dug out the roadbed and laid the oak railroad ties. When big tongs set the long steel rails in place, four or five men would hammer spikes into the steel plates. Harvey Sykes, Hale Curran's father, is one of the men in photograph. None of them are identified.

RAILROAD TRACKS IN TEMECULA CANYON. When the railroad engineers designed the route through the Temecula Canyon in 1882, the local people told them it was not a good idea because of possible flooding. The engineers researched weather patterns and declared there would be no problem. The tracks were rebuilt after they washed out in 1884 but were abandoned after washing out again in 1891.

SANTA FE RAILROAD TRACKS AFTER FLOOD, FEBRUARY 1927. These tracks were in the aptly named Railroad Canyon between present-day Canyon Lake and Lake Elsinore. The route originally ran from Colton to National City, south of San Diego. After the tracks were abandoned in the Temecula Canyon, the rail line continued from Colton to Temecula, where a turntable moved the train around to head back to Colton.

CALIFORNIA SOUTHERN RAILROAD DEPOT IN MURRIETA. Initially, the Murrieta depot was just a boxcar at the side of the tracks, but after the town site was surveyed, it was decided Murrieta would be a "meal depot" with a hotel. The Fountain House Hotel was built in 1885 to serve dinner as well as to accommodate overnight guests, and the depot house was constructed in 1887. After the depot was demolished, Walter Thompson used the lumber to build his home at Kalmia Street and Washington Avenue.

THE NOON TRAIN AT THE MURRIETA DEPOT, 1912. The bus to the left carried guests directly to and from Guenthers' Murrieta Hot Springs four miles away over scenic terrain. The bus, able to accommodate 25 passengers, met trains at the Murrieta Station twice a day.

THE CALIFORNIA SOUTHERN LINE LOCOMOTIVE NO. 14, C. 1890. This train ran from San Bernardino, through Murrieta and Temecula, then through the canyon, and finally on to National City, south of San Diego. The engine was propelled by steam from a boiler heated by a wood fire. The brass bell rang to call passengers before leaving the station. The train was stopped in front of the Bay View Saloon in National City.

MURRIETA TRAIN DEPOT AND CROSSING ON B STREET. The train ran through Murrieta until overland trucking replaced rail shipping. In 1935, the Santa Fe Company sent a work train through to remove the tracks. The workmen threw the oak ties aside and sold them for 10¢ each. For many years, railroad spikes littered the old roadbed.

FOUNTAIN HOUSE HOTEL WITH TRAIN, C. 1888. This photograph, taken from near the Murrieta Depot, shows the large size of the hotel and its closeness to the train. The roof of the Fox Bank is faintly visible over the train's fuel car. (Photograph courtesy of Historical Collection, Union Title Insurance Company, San Diego, California.)

SKETCH OF FOUNTAIN HOUSE HOTEL. The sketch shows the layout of the hotel in detail, with the outbuildings, the lightning rod, the windmill, tank house, and the fountain to the right of the building. The lightning rod was installed by Midwesterners who, unfamiliar with weather in Southern California, designed the hotel like they would in other states. The Santa Rosa Mountains frame the background with the notch in the mountains, known to locals as "The Dip," to the right of the windmill.

FOUNTAIN HOUSE WITH HORSE AND WAGON, C. 1900. The rider on horseback is identified as Gene Miller. At one time, a sign at the Fountain House advertised, "Feed and Stables for Horses of Guests." The Fountain House provided lodging for early land speculators and later for an overflow of guests from Guenthers' Murrieta Hot Springs Resort.

KATIE SLEEPER, HALE SYKES, AND GEORGE HALE AT FOUNTAIN HOUSE, 1912. Katie Sleeper was the proprietor of the hotel. Hale Sykes inherited the structure and used it as a residence. After the hotel burned down in 1935, the community pulled together to build a new home for Hale and her children. The home is still standing. Katie's nephew George Hale was later the barber at Guenthers' Murrieta Hot Springs.

A PLACE LIKE HOME

Fountain House

MRS. K. E. SLEEPER, PROP.

TERMS TO SUIT THE TIMES

OPPOSITE DEPOT   MURRIETTA, CAL.

KATIE SLEEPER'S BUSINESS CARD. Her card announced, "A Place Like Home," and "Terms to Suit the Times." The hotel was painted a shade of peach and trimmed in chocolate brown. Inside the guest rooms were decorated with wallpaper in pastel patterns. Room rates were 50¢ a night.

HALE AND HER FRIEND "PUTSY," JUNE 19, 1919. The concrete base of the fountain at the Fountain House Hotel provided a pleasant place to sit on a hot afternoon. The photograph, taken toward the northeast, caught the caboose as it passed the hotel on the Atchison, Topeka and Santa Fe Line. Hale and Putsy rode horseback together. The fountain base is still standing.

SIDE YARD OF FOUNTAIN HOUSE HOTEL, 1896. Before television and video games, the Sykes family entertained themselves with a game of croquet, while Dave Buchanan watched from his bicycle in back left corner. The Sykes, from left to right, are Mabel, Harvey, Walter, Lois, Grandma Sykes, Ollie, Rose, and Jane.

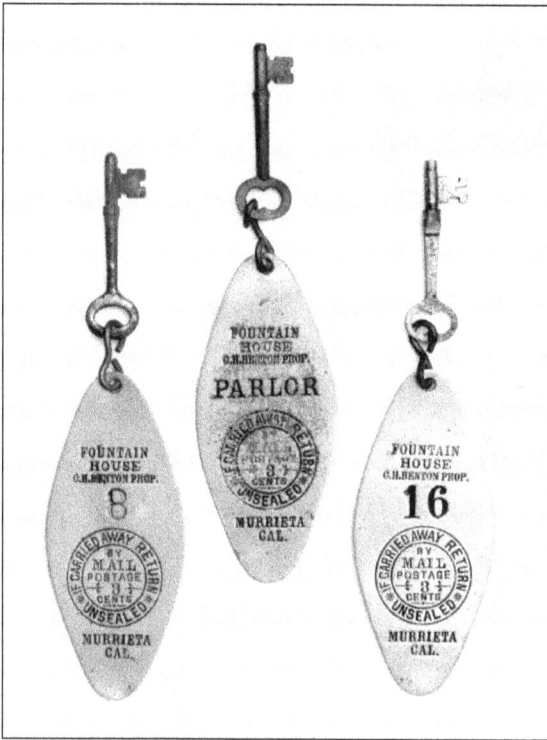

KEYS TO FOUNTAIN HOUSE HOTEL. Guest rooms were numbered 9 through 17. Superstitious clients would not stay in room 13, so the number "3" was cleverly painted with two loops to turn it into an "8." Before plastic cards were issued as keys to hotel rooms, a guest who left the hotel with keys could return them without an envelope for 3¢ postage.

FOUNTAIN HOUSE MEAL TICKET. The Fountain House was known for its good home-cooked food, which was served promptly and at reasonable prices three times a day. As a railroad stop, the hotel was patronized for its food as much as it was for lodging. People would flock to the hotel on Sundays for the 35¢ chicken dinner, and they would eat like they had not had food for a week.

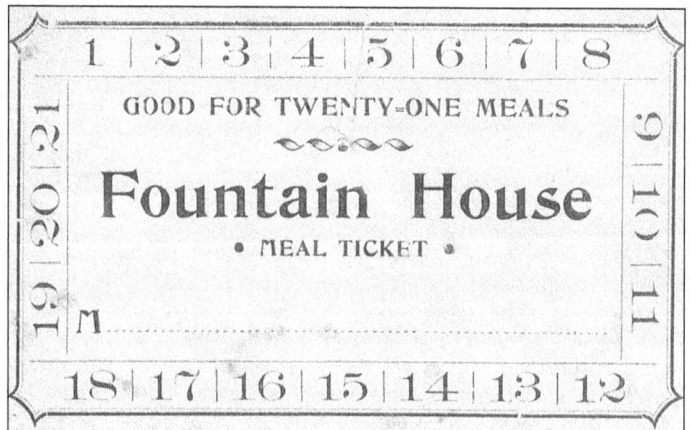

GOOD FOR TWENTY-ONE MEALS

Fountain House

• MEAL TICKET •

Two

EARLY FARM COMMERCE

BERT BAXTER WITH SACKS OF GRAIN. Baxter's heavily loaded wagons carried sacks of grain to the train after harvest. Murrieta farmers packed about 100,000 sacks of grain each season, but empty grain bags cost 27¢ each and were hard to find. When the grain elevator was built, the farmers could reuse their bags after emptying the grain at the elevator. Baxter's farm was on what is now called Baxter Road.

MURRIETA'S DISPLAY AT THE RIVERSIDE COUNTY FAIR, 1913. This is Murrieta's display at the Riverside County Fair in 1913, when Murrieta took first prize at Fairmont Park in Riverside. Mary Rail made the signs from seeds, alfalfa, barley, and honey. Murrieta was known for its fruits and other produce.

MURRIETA'S EXHIBIT AT THE COUNTY FAIR. The Murrieta Chamber of Commerce publicized the town as "the great dry-farming district of Riverside County." With irrigation in the 1920s, Murrieta lettuce was shipped to Chicago and New York by train, giving a profit of $1,500 per boxcar load.

MURRIETA MEAT MARKET WAGON, 1886. Before automobiles, and when stores were few and far between, peddlers went to the customer's door. This peddler sold meat—mutton, pork, beef, cured meats, and sausage—from a Baldwin and Bonham wagon.

GEORGE FEZLER AND VEGETABLE WAGON, C. 1911. Fezler, third from left, sold homegrown vegetables, making a route from San Bernardino to Valley Center. His wife ran a lunch stand by the Murrieta Train Depot to service passengers on the noon train. Fezler was considered a smooth talker who could talk anyone into or out of anything. His adopted son Frank had a reputation of picking up anything that wasn't nailed down but would return it when asked. The Fezlers are buried in Laurel Cemetery.

THRESHING, EARLY 1900S. This Bakersfield photograph shows equipment typical to harvest crews of the era. The steam engine that powered the thresher was separated from the grain by a long belt to prevent fire from igniting the crop.

THRESHING, EARLY 1900S. Processing 30 sacks of grain was considered a good day's work. It was hard labor on a hot day, with chaff blowing in the workers' eyes and irritating their skin. Men who owned threshing machines hired out to work other farmers' fields.

BALING HAY AT BAXTER'S FARM. The photograph, looking south, shows the accomplishments of a long day's work as shadows lengthen. A platform scale weighed bales up to 200 pounds. A workday began at sunup and ended at sundown. To the right of the horses, a small campfire heated coffee in a tin can.

STACKING BALES OF HAY, EARLY 1900s. The process went as pictured from left to right. First the hay was cut before being carried in a wagon to the baling area, where men with pitchforks loaded the baler. The bales were then tied with baling wire and were put into a tall stack covered by corrugated sheet metal to keep it from being ruined by rain.

31

CHARNOCK RANCH, EARLY 1900S. This was a typical ranch of the era with cattle and horses, wagons, and barns. It was located at the southeast corner of Murrieta Hot Springs Road and

THE GEORGE LAMBERTS, C. 1906. This photograph was taken in front of George Lambert's barn on his 340-acre ranch south of Guava Street. The family, in their Sunday best, display their two horses and carriage, barn, windmill, and sizable head of cattle. The little girl shows her wagon

Jefferson Avenue. Murrieta Hot Springs Road was renamed Webster Avenue in the 1950s to help visitors find Guenthers' Murrieta Hot Springs Resort more easily.

and her doll carriage. Lambert, a dairy farmer, left cans of cream on the platform at the Linda Rosa stop for the train to take to Riverside.

HARVESTING IN FRENCH VALLEY, THE 1920S. Brothers Juan and Eulogio Sotello, the first Murrieta residents to move to the town from Mexico, worked "the baling and harvesting circuit" doing custom baling for harvesting crews in the area. Sixteen-year-old Juan came from Guanojuato in 1900, and his brother Eulogio arrived in 1922. Juan bought the property still owned by the family at the corner of Ivy and Second Streets. (Photograph courtesy of the Sotello family.)

HARVESTER AND SIX-MAN CREW, 1894. Henry C. Thompson owned the first combine harvester in this part of the county. The machine simplified the threshing process and required fewer workers.

THE OLD HUTCHINSON BARN, 1971. The barn is still standing at Washington Avenue and Brown Street. The ramp on the left side is a cattle loader to drive the cattle into a transport vehicle. Albert Hutchinson originally leased land from Juan Murrieta and partnered with William Brown in a dairy operation.

TWO HORSES IN THE PROVOLT BARN, 1930. Hale Curran wrote on the back of the photograph, "The last horses daddy had to work the ranch." The Provolt Place at the corner of Guava Street and Jefferson Avenue was originally owned by the Merrills. The barn is no longer standing.

VERNON JAMES'S WATER WAGON. "Vernie" James worked as a foreman for the county road department and rented his water wagon for use in constructing roads. He was also one of the primary supporters for the building of the Murrieta Grain Elevator. Six horses pulled the wagon. Notice the bells on the lead horses.

HARVESTER PULLED BY HORSES. T. R. Wickerd's crew harvested grain across the creek from town with the dip in the mountains in the background. An umbrella provided shade for the harvester, which is in contrast to modern combines that feature air-conditioned cabs.

TEAMSTER WITH SIX MULES AND PLOW. This farmer had been hard at work, as seen by the plowed land in the background. Mules, the offspring of female horses and male donkeys, bore heavy responsibility in farming. Some farmers preferred mules to horses because of their resistance to disease and their strong endurance.

STEAM TRACTOR. This tractor, powered by a steam engine, featured a boiler in front. The men were dwarfed by its massive size. The metal-wheeled tractor pulled a combine in the middle of a grain field.

CARS IN THE SILICA MINE, C. 1990. A silica mine, located near present-day Clinton Keith Road and Interstate 215, operated from 1922 to 1933 and produced nearly pure silica. Local men, including Eulogio Sotello, a driller and blaster, worked the mine. When water was pumped out of the old mine to build a housing tract, workers found 40 abandoned cars.

THE STILE BELOW LAMBERT'S RANCH, 1976. The stile, a ladder over the fence, was a landmark between the towns of Temecula and Murrieta in an area called the Linda Rosa. In 1888, a developer built a beautiful hotel to attract speculators to the Linda Rosa, but his timing was poor, and the land didn't sell. The Linda Rosa development was doomed, and the hotel was torn down. Eli Barnett purchased the salvaged materials to build his home in Temecula.

CONSTRUCTION OF THE GRAIN ELEVATOR, AUGUST 1, 1918. Before the elevator was erected, farmers took grain to a warehouse at Clay Avenue and B Street. Buyers bought bags of grain and shipped it to mills by train. A shortage of grain bags prompted the local farmers to form the Murrieta Valley Grain Elevator Company and sell $50 shares to build the concrete elevator. When the elevator opened, loaded farm wagons formed long lines along Clay Avenue, waiting to deposit their grain.

THE MURRIETA GRAIN ELEVATOR, 1958. The 96-foot-tall elevator stood next to the railroad tracks near the depot. It was sometimes called the Murrieta Sentinel. While the elevator was under construction, an entertainer climbed to the top of the tower and did gymnastic acts for the crowd waiting for the evening mail train. In 1991, after several decades of declining need for grain storage, the elevator was boarded up. It still stands as a reminder of the past.

OLD COOK SHACK BY THE JOY HOUSE. Cook shacks on wheels, like this one, are seen in several of the harvesting photographs in this book. They were like chuck wagons that were used by cowboys but were larger to allow cooking inside so food was safe from flies and blowing chaff. This cook shack sat across from RCP Concrete Works on Jefferson Avenue between Elm and Fig Streets until the late 1990s.

Three

EARLY PEOPLE AND BUSINESSES

WILLIAM AND MARTHA BROWN'S FARM, 1894. This house is at the corner of Brown Street and Adams Avenue. A long ladder reached to a door at the top of the barn where hay bales were loaded. Brown and Albert Hutchinson ran a dairy south of Murrieta at the former homestead of Juan Murrieta. Their cows were branded "HB."

MILES AND SARAH BUCHANAN THOMPSON AND SON MEVILLE, 1895. The family sat in front of their home on the land they cleared and improved in French Valley. The fencing kept animals out. They worked hard as evidenced by the pile of logs on the far side of their home and the shrubbery planted. A wringer washer on the front porch was a prized possession and status symbol compared to the lowly scrub boards and washtubs used by others. The outhouse was discretely hidden behind bushes to the far right.

ROUGHING IT IN EARLY MURRIETA. This mother, three children, and a dog pose proudly in front of their home. Perhaps the deep *metate*, a Native American grinding stone, was found near their house. They had precious firewood stacked on their porch and the girl had a pretty doll. The boys' shirts were made from the same bolt of cloth.

THE HEDGES PLACE. J. C. Rail poses with his children in front of the home they bought on the southeast corner of Washington Avenue and Ivy Street from Marcus and Emma Hedges in 1906. The house was constructed in 1900 from clear redwood, a fine quality of wood that was termite resistant. The Rail children, pictured from left to right, are Ira, Freda, Floyd, and Verna. School classes met in the lean-to of the barn on this property while the first grammar school was under construction.

INSIDE THE RAIL HOME. While Mabel Irey lived in the house, the home was decorated with Victorian décor typical of the early 20th century, with an ornate pump organ and kerosene lamp. A portrait of Henry Thompson, Mabel's father, hung to the left side of the window. Thompson, a widower, came to Murrieta from Kansas with six children in 1887. He served as Riverside County Supervisor for a number of years.

43

LAKEMANS ICE CREAM PARLOR AND HOME, 1909. The sign advertises cigars, tobacco, and ice cream. The house was built in 1895 for the A. B. Burnetts and was later the residence of

LAKEMANS LUNCH ROOM. Signs on this café in the center of Murrieta's business district advertise meals at all hours, Folgers Golden Gate Coffee, Tom Keene Cigars, Hub City Laundry Agency, and a bakery. It was known as an ice cream and soda parlor. The Lakemans owned a five-acre orchard that produced pears, apples, cherries, figs, and nectarines.

Henry Thompson. The ice cream parlor became Ray's Murrieta Café, a familiar place along Washington Avenue that welcomed residents and travelers on Highway 395. Both buildings are still standing.

THE LAKEMAN HOUSE. Mrs. Lakeman, Jim Witcher, Mr. Lakeman, and the Lakemans' grandson Elmer Louden pose with a dog in front of their home on Washington Avenue, between B Street and Juniper Street. The home, built in 1885 by Daniel Buchanan, is still standing.

BENJAMIN WYLIE TARWATER'S HOME ON PLUM STREET. Mr. Tarwater hosed the lawn, while his wife, Nancy, watched Urban, Earl, and Alda. The Tarwaters built this home in 1888. Tarwater had his eye on Murrieta for several years before Juan Murrieta would sell any land. Tarwater originally worked at a general store in Cuyamaca in San Diego County. As he prospered, he opened new stores in Julian and then in Murrieta.

RENOVATED TARWATER HOUSE, 2006. Ayleen Gibbo, a Murrieta resident concerned with historic preservation, bought the Tarwater House and since 1986 has renovated it to its present charm.

BUNKHOUSE AT SOTELLO HOMESTEAD, C. 1975. Eulogio Sotello provided this bunkhouse, made from a railroad boxcar, for workers he employed to do custom farming, hay baling, and threshing from French Valley to Winchester. The workers from Pechanga and Pala also helped pick walnuts from Elsinore groves. (Photograph courtesy of the Sotello family.)

NETTIE LLOYD'S HOUSE. Nettie poses in front of her house that is still standing at the corner of Juniper and First Streets. Her husband raised bees and farmed.

WALTER AND SADIE THOMPSONS' HOME. Sadie's father, David Buchanan, built this house on the east side of Washington Avenue. Walter's brother Meville, a farmer and constable, lived on the next hill. The house was torn down when an adobe house, made from local clay, was built at the top of the hill.

THE DOOLITTLE HOUSE. This home on Juniper Street was the first built in Murrieta. Daniel Buchanan wrote in his diary that he and A. R. Doolittle, experienced carpenters who also built the Methodist church, constructed the house in 10 days. Doolittle's Clothing and Millinery opened in 1888 over the Murrieta Drug Store. Miss Billy Riley renovated the house in 1973. It is now an antique store.

THE HAMILTON HOUSE. This beautiful home graces Washington Avenue in the heart of Murrieta's historic downtown. Jack Hamilton, a quality builder, constructed this home and also built the Murrieta Post Office. The home is now owned by Jack and Rina Hamilton's daughter Winifred Tubbs.

THE GARRISON HOME. Victor "Vic" Garrison bought the seven acres at the corner of Washington Avenue and C Street in 1938. The Murrieta Machine Shop and the home where he and Arlean were married in 1940 were built 10 years earlier. Both the machine shop and the house are still standing. Vic was Murrieta Volunteer Fire Department's first assistant chief and was one of the original 10 volunteers. Arlean wrote for local newspapers and penned *My Children's Home*, a book about Murrieta.

THE DANIEL N. BUCHANAN HOME. Buchanan came from Nebraska in 1884 and was the first settler to buy lots in the Murrieta town site. He was a rancher, contractor, carpenter, and builder. He made and sold fencing material and installed two types of windmills. Buchanan built several homes and buildings in Murrieta. In this photograph, someone is displaying the strong water pressure in the garden hose, perhaps to sell the qualities of a good windmill.

THE PROVOLT HOUSE ON JEFFERSON AVENUE. This photograph, taken on the corner of Jefferson Avenue and Guava Street, shows a typical ranch of the area with a craftsman house, an umbrella tree, a windmill, a water tank, and a barn surrounded by open fields. The buildings are gone. The Tenaja Grade and "The Dip" are visible in the backdrop formed by the Santa Rosa Mountains.

SYKES'S RANCH. Henry and Sarah Sykes brought their nine children to California in 1890 from Kansas. Three more children were born to the Sykes while they were the proprietors of the Fountain House Hotel from 1890 to 1907. Their later home on a 154-acre ranch north of Tenaja Road on Hayes Avenue was recently demolished after it was vandalized and fell into disrepair.

JOHN AND SARAH DUNHAMS' HOME. The couple came from the Midwest in 1913 and bought 10 acres of land between B and Kalmia Streets where they built their home. The house burned down in the 1930s. Their son Lawrence and his wife, Lucy, operated a gas station and grocery store at the corner of Washington Avenue and A Street. Lawrence was one of the 10 original volunteer firemen. Lawrence's brother Elmo worked on road construction most of his life.

THE GARRISON HOME. H. S. Garrison, no relation to Vic and Arlean Garrison, built and furnished this beautiful Craftsman home. He landscaped the property and planted fruit trees on both sides of his driveway.

THE GARRISON RANCH. Garrison, a partner in a clay mine in Linda Rosa, planted an olive grove along Hayes Avenue, extending from Juniper to Ivy Streets, where it ended across from Laurel Cemetery. Garrison produced olive oil and shipped it to markets around the country.

INSIDE THE GARRISON DINING ROOM. Gas carbide lights illuminated the home before electrical power was available. The gas valves are located under each light on the chandelier.

INSIDE THE GARRISON PARLOR. The furniture and rugs in the home of this successful businessman were expensive treasures. The Navajo rug in the dining room, the complete animal furs, and other furnishings were not typical to farm homes of the area. The house and everything in it burned during a fire in the 1930s.

THE OLD JOY HOUSE. This once solid home stood next to Urban Tarwater's reservoir on Jefferson Avenue. After many years of neglect, the house was torn down. For quite a while, the old cook shack and windmill remained as ghosts of the past along Jefferson Avenue.

Four

COMMERCE OF THE 20TH CENTURY

M. MOONEY'S BLACKSMITH AND WAGON SHOP. This stood at the corner of Washington Avenue and B Street and was later the site of the Tarwater Store. To the left is "Dad" Ashley, and one of the men is identified as Mooney. The other is not identified. The two younger men are wearing leather aprons to protect themselves from burning at the "smithy."

THE NEW HIGHWAY, 1917. The transition from horse-and-buggy to motorcar brought demands for smoother roads. Washington Avenue was paved in 1917, and the highway extended through Jefferson Avenue into Temecula. The business district of Murrieta shifted from the area around the train depot to along the new highway on Washington Avenue.

DOC STURGES IN THE BACK SEAT OF HIS TWO–PASSENGER CAR. Jim Witcher stood beside the unusual car, with room for one in front and one in back, at the Murrietta Garage. The garage sold Red Crown gasoline, a predecessor of Standard Oil. Dr. John Sturges came to Murrieta in 1899 after graduating from Rush Medical College in Chicago. He practiced medicine in Murrieta for over 30 years.

A. K. SMALL AND SON'S ASSOCIATED GAS STATION, 1935. A. K. "Bert" Small, a native of Maine, was a partner with his father-in-law, Henry Thompson, in a general mercantile store before opening this gas station. Bert served as postmaster from 1928 through 1936, while the post office was located in his store. He was also town librarian and secretary for the elevator company. The prefabricated building was constructed of lumber held together in the center by a long steel rod and chains.

CURRAN'S ASSOCIATED STATION, GARAGE, AND GREYHOUND BUS STOP. By the time Marvin Curran bought the former Small gas station at the corner of Washington Avenue and Juniper Street from Eldon Knott in 1950, the old pumps with glass reservoirs were replaced with modern electric pumps. Curran later closed the station and purchased one at Ivy Street and Jefferson Avenue.

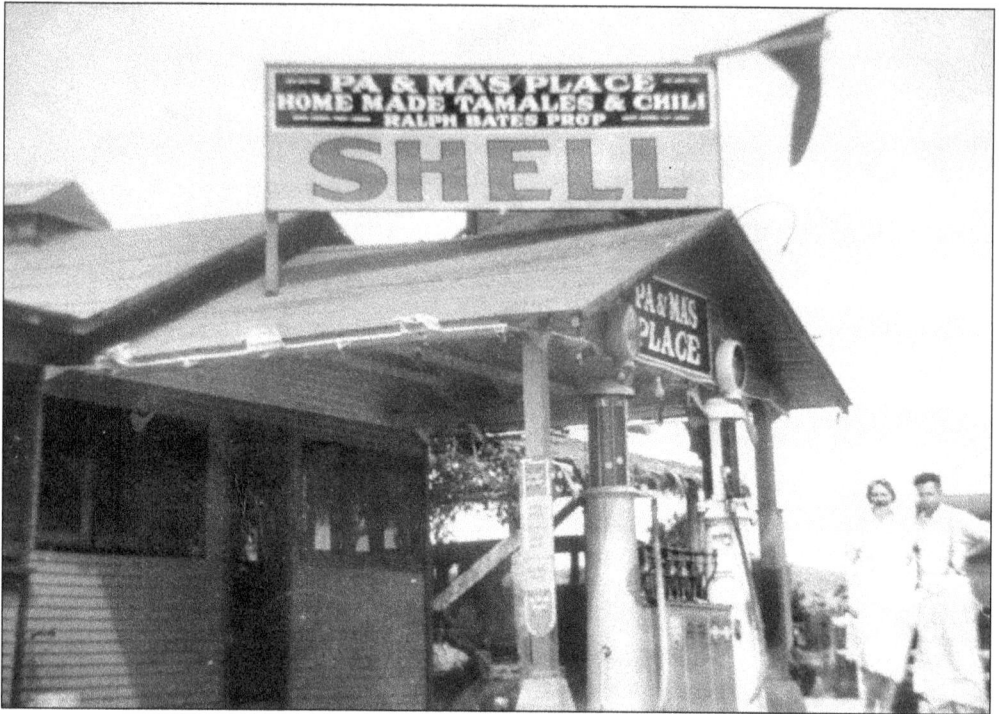

PA AND MA BATES'S GAS STATION AND RESTAURANT, 1929. Ma and Pa Bates stand in front of their business. The gas station and restaurant were open 24 hours a day. They served tamales with chili and beans for 25¢, a rib eye steak for 50¢, and a T-bone steak for 75¢. They did short orders, too, but the establishment was especially known for their good *chili con carne*.

MARVIN CURRAN AT THE MURRIETA MACHINE SHOP, THE 1940s. The machine shop was the center of city business and activity, and for many years, it was considered the unofficial town hall, largely due to Arlean Garrison's involvement in the community. Vic Garrison sold farm implements during the war, and after the war, he repaired machinery and did welding. Curran tells about fabricating things for secretive inventors while he worked there.

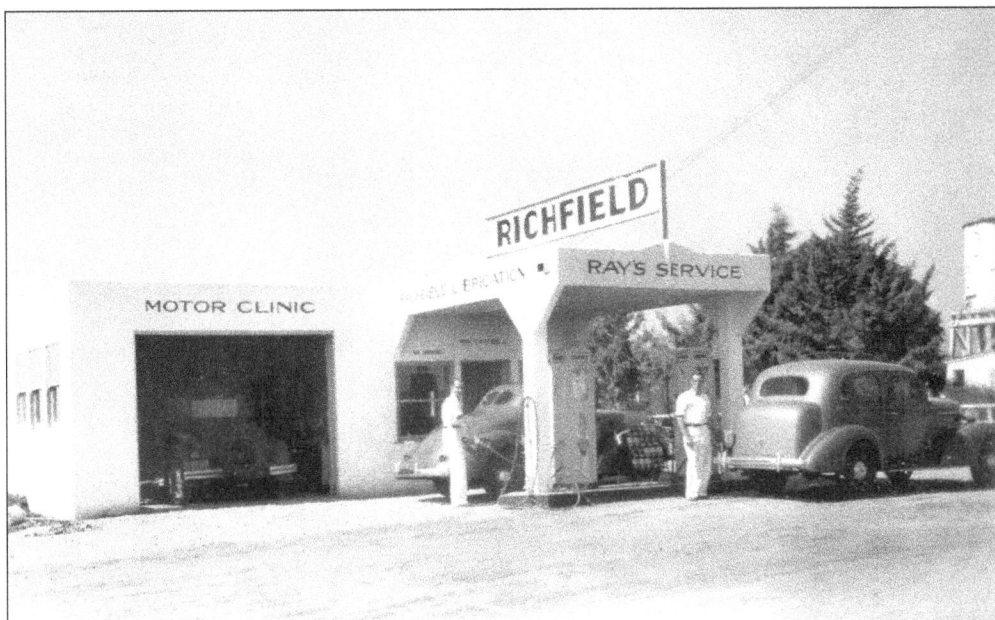

Ray's Richfield Gas Station, November 1938. This station, owned by Daniel Raymond Campbell Jr., sat on Ivy Street near Jefferson Avenue and across from the barn painted with advertisements for Reno and Temecula Hot Springs.

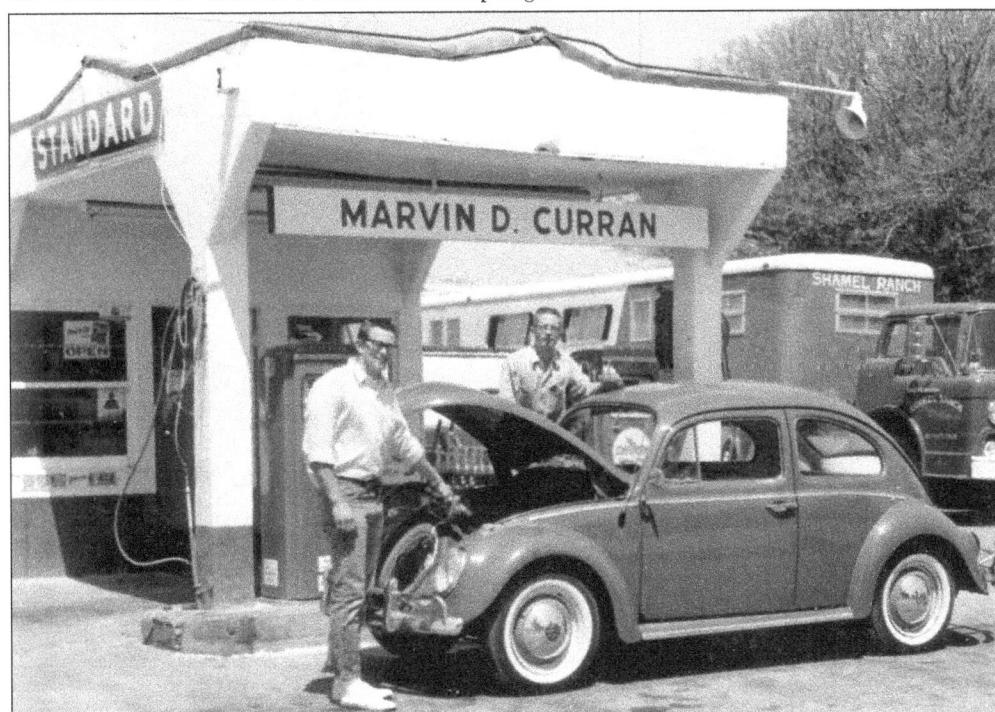

Marvin Curran at His Standard Gas Station and Garage on Ivy Street, 1960. This is the same station as pictured above. When Max Thompson owned the station, he sold Chevron gasoline. Thompson sold to Clayton Erdel, Loretta Barnett's father, and Curran bought it from Erdel. The building was demolished in April 2006.

THE B. W. TARWATER CASH STORE. The sign announced it was a "cash store," meaning that no one could put goods on an account to pay off later. It does indicate that goods could be exchanged for produce. Several store ledgers kept during this era in neighboring towns indicate that farmers exchanged grain, eggs, chicken, or produce for goods. Old-timers remember that Tarwater did allow goods on credit, and many paid their debts with land in an area later called Tarwater Flats.

THE MURRIETA HARDWARE STORE, 1918. Signs on this store owned by B. W. Tarwater advertised Dr. J. A. Sturges's Drugs, Oliver Plows, and Tom Keene Cigars. Pictured in front, from left to right, are an unidentified boy, Doc Sturges (who lived in the lean-to), an unidentified man, William Anderson (sitting) and Ezra Cocking, the Methodist minister. People gathered at the store to play checkers and share gossip.

DOC LASHLEE'S DRUG STORE ON THIRD AVENUE. This photograph was taken on a cold day when even the horse needed a blanket. In the background, the "old blue barn" on Second Street and the house of George Fox, the banker, are visible. This, the first drugstore in town, was home to the Murrieta Post Office before it was moved to the train depot. Dr. Horace Lashlee served as Murrieta's first postmaster. The blue barn was destroyed by fire in 1908.

THE AINSWORTH AND FALLIS GENERAL MERCHANDISE STORE, CLAY STREET. Brothers William and John Colerick opened a store in a tent here next to the hotel between A and B Streets in 1885. They sold to Ainsworth and Fallis in 1895. George Fox's bank was to the left of the store. The sign on the hitching rail advertised Morris' Poultry Cure. The other signs advertised biscuits, gentlemen's suits, and Deere Harvesting Machinery.

THE TARWATER STORE, C. 1917. The 48- by 60-foot general merchandise store was built facing B Street around 1916. This was the most important street in Murrieta, connecting the town to the depot and hotel. The store was second only to Colerick Brothers as the oldest mercantile business in the valley. A blacksmith shop stood at the location previously.

THE TARWATER STORE AND TOKENS FOR BILLIARDS, 1917. Washington Avenue, in the foreground, was paved during the transition from horse-and-buggy to the horseless carriage. The building by the windmill was the town hall, and the pool hall was on the south side of B Street. Tokens from the Brunswick Balke Collender Company were good for 10¢ of trade at the Jules Escallier's Billiard Hall.

OLD DOC LASHLEE'S DRUG STORE. Signs decorating this wood building advertised a feed store for poultry, "live stock," Taylor's Products, and Barnett's Store. After Doc Lashlee's Drug Store went out of business, the elevator company used the building as an office. In the 1940s and 1950s, it was used for hay storage.

MURRIETA TOWN HALL. This building, constructed in 1903, was called the town hall or historic hall. The structure on B Street provided a community social center where meetings and dances were held. A large chalkboard in the front of the hall publicized town events. The hall was demolished after a fire destroyed it in 1924.

BAKER JOHN BEELER SHOWS HIS LOAVES, 1914. John Beeler's bakery sat at Winters Corner on Washington Avenue and B Street across from the Tarwater or Burnham Store. The town blackboard was moved to his bakery after the town hall burned and later was moved to the post office. Beeler was the founding president of the Murrieta Chamber of Commerce in 1917.

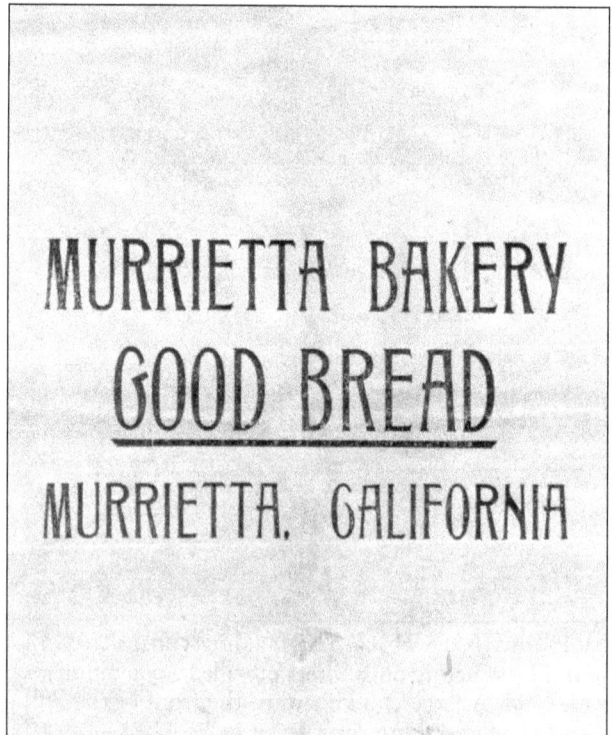

MURRIETTA BAKERY
GOOD BREAD
MURRIETTA, CALIFORNIA

GOOD BREAD BAKERY ADVERTISEMENT. The sands of time have eroded both the paper of this ad and also any recollection of where the bakery was or who owned it. Because the advertisement features two "T"s, one would suppose the bakery was in business before 1924, when the correction was made to the incorrect spelling in the original post office application of 1885.

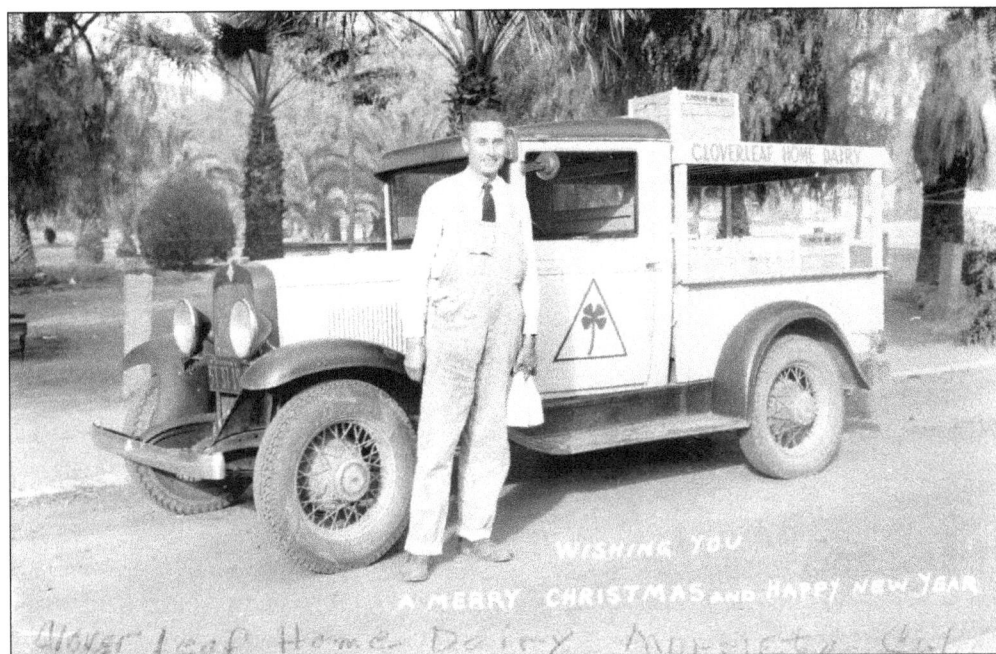

CLOVERLEAF HOME DAIRY CHRISTMAS POSTCARD GREETING. Milkmen made daily home deliveries of dairy products. The milk came in glass bottles with cardboard stoppers, and empty bottles were picked up and reused by the dairy. The Cloverleaf Dairy was at the west end of Juniper Street. As the very successful business grew, they delivered throughout the valley and eventually relocated to Wildomar.

JESSE AND EULOGIO SOTELLO, C. 1937. Eulogio was disabled from silicosis after drilling and blasting for several years in the Murrieta silica mine. When he couldn't walk anymore, he made a wheelchair for himself. Jessie supported the family by working as a seamstress in a factory in Elsinore. The children worked on farm crews, raised rabbits, and cut firewood. (Photograph courtesy of the Sotello family.)

THE JOHN M. RICHARDSON BUILDING. This business on First Street, near B Street, sold farm implements and painting supplies. A cat guarded the door to the post office service counter. Richardson served as school clerk and postmaster. An unusual windmill stood behind the living quarters that were decorated with lace curtains and warmed by a stove. The Methodist church on A Street is to the left.

MURRIETA POST OFFICE, 1948. Jack Hamilton constructed this 700-square-foot building at Washington Avenue and C Street in 1940 on property he owned. The facility served the population well until Murrieta's growth spurt during the 1980s. A new post office was dedicated in 1985 to serve the growing community.

Hale Curran in the Murrieta Post Office. Hale walked to her job at Guenthers' Murrieta Hot Springs from her home near the Murrieta elevator until Rose Tarwater, the newly appointed postmistress, invited her to take a job as clerk at the post office. Hale made 50¢ a day at the hot springs. She started for less money at the post office but didn't have to walk as far to work.

Murrieta Post Office, 1963. When Hale Curran began working for the Murrieta Post Office in 1936, it was in a dark corner of the A. K. Small Store. Hale saw a lot of changes in the post office before she retired in 1966. She moved to the new post office in 1940 and learned to use new equipment as technology changed. She watched the population grow with increased demands on postal service. This photograph shows Hale with Dixie Ely and Rose Tarwater.

ALBERT K. SMALL'S STORE. The store, built at the corner of Washington Avenue and Juniper Street in 1908, housed the post office from 1928 to 1940. This photograph was taken before Washington Avenue was paved in 1917. The Birdsell Wagon business was to the right of the building. The trees were used for posting signs, and a stump in the center was used as a kiosk for El Portana Cigars.

A. K. SMALL'S GROCERY AND HARDWARE STORE, MAY 5, 1917. The sign to the right advertised Weber Wagons and another sign advertised Star Tobacco. A buggy pulled by a burro hid behind a tree to the left. Boxes of merchandise piled in front of the store indicated a brisk business. The men, from left to right, are Henry Thompson, Doc Sturges, A. K. Small, and Harry Thompson.

BURNHAM'S STORE, C. 1958. A. K. Small sold his general store in 1922 to George Burnham and his son Frank. During the 1950s, each purchase in Burnham's Store earned a few Orange Stamps. Orange Stamps were pasted into booklets and redeemed for merchandise like electric skillets, irons, percolators, or card tables. Judge Hilliard held court in the south end of the building.

WASHINGTON AVENUE AND JUNIPER STREET, C. 1968. This building was an antique store when the photograph was taken. Today it is a donut shop. Rays Café, to the right, was originally Lakemans Ice Cream Parlor. Later the Eilers owned it and sold it to the Bezansons.

MURRIETA METHODIST CHURCH. The first preacher who came to Murrieta held classes at the Fountain House Hotel in April 1885. Daniel Buchanan built the Methodist church shortly after the congregation organized in 1886. The first pastor, Rev. Amos Ogburn, fell from the roof while painting, and Buchanan made him a pair of crutches. The minister lived in the house to the right.

LATER PHOTOGRAPH OF MURRIETA METHODIST CHURCH. Reverend Ogburn was assigned to both the Winchester and Murrieta Methodist Churches, so he alternated weeks between the two. On Sundays when there was no worship service in Murrieta, a layperson taught Sunday school. Although the land for the church cost $140 and the construction cost $2,000, the church was debt free in 1887.

RUBBLE FROM THE MURRIETA CHURCH FIRE, 1963. Clara Edwards awakened early on April 10 to see fire on the roof of the church and called Vic Garrison, who lived near the fire station. Firemen saved the parsonage but could not save the church from the arsonist's fire. The following Sunday was Easter, and services were held at the Sykes Ranch as the congregation planned to rebuild the church.

RALPH LOVE'S PAINTING OF THE MURRIETA METHODIST CHURCH. Mrs. Love showed the painting by her husband Ralph Love, a talented painter who found inspiration in the scenes of the region. Octavia Curran owned this painting and donated it to the church. It is presently displayed in the new church that was built on Kalmia Street and Adams Avenue in 1965.

MOTHER'S DAY AT MURRIETA METHODIST CHURCH, 1931. Notice the white corsages worn by daughters whose mothers were gone and colored corsages worn by women whose mothers were still living. Pictured here, from left to right, are (first row) Edith Small, Mrs. Saxman, Blanche Thompson, Vera Knott, Freda Knott, Mary Rail, and Sarah Jane Parker; (second row) Reverend Grandy, Emma Compton, Alda Wickerd, Nellie Thompson, Nettie Lloyd, Sadie Thompson, Hazel Rail, Mabel Crews, and Dovie Sykes; (third row) Myrtle Roripaugh, Rose Tarwater, Cora Coleman, and Mrs. Cook.

THE FIRST HOLINESS CHURCH. The church stood at the corner of B and First Streets. Six members of the William Bradford and David Buchanan families organized the church in 1886. The original building burned and was rebuilt at the same location. The revival-style services were loud enough to be heard by people in neighboring homes. Hale Sykes Curran was born in a house behind the church in 1900.

THE EPISCOPAL CHURCH, 2006. The congregation purchased the land in 1886 for $140. Since the Episcopal congregation disbanded, the building has been home to several different church denominations and is still in use today.

Casket Bill for Services, June 25, 1894. Robert Bollen, a carpenter, wrote to ask M. W. Thompson for $17, "I Would not Send this Bill But I have not been Able to Doo a days Work for over three Weeks and am in grate Nead of Som Money and you Will gratly Oblige me By Paying the above Bill if Posible. Yours Truly, R. W. Bollen."

Judge William Thorne. Thorne was Murrieta's first justice of the peace and judge, serving from 1917 to 1940. A portion of A. K. Small's building was reserved for the Murrieta court. His home was on Adams Avenue.

Five

SPECIAL PEOPLE AND LOCATIONS

THE CYCLIST. With determination popping out the veins on his neck, the cyclist focused straight ahead while his buddy supported the bike. His scuffed ankle testifies to earlier attempts to keep the bike upright, and practice taught them to start near a wall. On the back of the photograph someone wrote, "Alex Matteson's brother on bicycle and Ester's uncle."

THE SANTA ROSA RANCH HOUSE. After a long drive on a dirt road winding through the hills northeast of Murrieta, this Victorian house and its floral landscaping was a beautiful destination. All the lumber was hauled up the Linda Rosa Grade and past the volcano rock near the Damian's Place when Parker Dear built the house in 1880. The house burned down in the 1970s, and the Nature Conservancy now owns the ranch.

PARKER DEAR'S HOUSE AT THE SANTA ROSA, 1887. Juan Moreno raised cattle here on the land he received from Gov. Pio Pico in the 1840s. Trees obscure the Moreno Adobe from view. Parker Dear's father was one of the Englishmen who invested in the property in 1876. Gordon House, a longtime resident of Murrieta, gave historical tours of the plateau to the public until his death in 2006.

MAY DAY PICNIC. City folk dined in style while seated on the ground in the pleasant pastureland of the Santa Rosa Ranch. Ladies sported fancy hats and gentlemen wore wildflower boutonnieres. An older man sat on a stump, while buggies and wagons waited in the background. The May Day Picnic was a big event each year.

INSTRUMENTALISTS ON BAND ROCK. This natural bandstand was used during May Day Picnics. The musicians in the photograph are unidentified. Mr. and Mrs. Parker Dear supplied the location, a beef, pig, and sheep, and each family provided potluck food. Committees organized transportation and sales of lemonade, coffee, and cake. Community leaders organized the event, and people were invited from Murrieta and neighboring communities.

YOUTH POSING AT THE SANTA ROSA, C. 1903. Pictured here, from left to right, are (first row) Tom Shrode, Charles Garrison, and Lester Black; (second row) Birdie Ainsworth, Stella Bogart, Dovie Miller, and Olive Sykes. A committee organized games and probably arranged for the photographer's services at this May Day Picnic.

PICNIC AT THE SANTA ROSA, C. 1903. This was taken at the same location on the same day as the top photograph and shows, once more, picnickers in their best summer party clothes at the Santa Rosa Rancho. The bearded man to the far right was Henry Thompson.

SANTA ROSA RANCH, C. 1903. The Santa Rosa Ranch features scenic serenity in various areas of repose. There are wooded areas shrouded by Engelmann Oaks and open grassy fields with neighboring patches of prickly pear cactus. Fish swim in crystal-clear pools and huge tarantulas creep along roadways. Now a nature preserve, visitors take in the beautiful scenery as they hike along trails to old adobe structures.

WADING AT THE SANTA ROSA RANCH, C. 1903. Nila Hadsall and Helen Hope couldn't resist taking off their shoes to cool their feet in a shady spot at the Santa Rosa Ranch during a May Day Picnic.

MURRIETA BASEBALL TEAM, EARLY 1900S. The Murrieta baseball team poses without uniforms but does display their early baseball equipment. They played against teams from Temecula and the Pala Reservation. Walter, Cliff, and Harry Thompson; Rex and Charlie Swain; Vernon James; and Leonard Smohl are in the photograph in no particular order. The others are not identified.

THE MURRIETA GNOMES, 1916. These future leaders of Murrieta were in costumes for an event long forgotten. Standing in a field with their backs to Washington Avenue, from left to right, are Max Thompson, Howard Diniwiddie, Carroll Kifer, Howard Black, Cecil Rail, Albert Small, and Alvin Chisman.

SITTING IN THE "FLIVER," 1912. Katie Sleeper, her niece Hale, and nephew George sit parked behind the Fountain House Hotel. During this era, a car was called "a machine," or more affectionately, "a fliver." Headlights were called "lamps." A toolbox sat on the running board and a fold-down top was common.

MURRIETA BACHELORS, 1914. The eligible men of town sit at a picnic table made from planks of wood supported by sawhorses and box crates. Pictured, from left to right, are Jack Baker, Herbert Olds, Theodore Jurberg, Bill Harvey, Mr. Rodriguez, Dave Buchanan, Wesley Freeman, Mr. Scott, Sam James, Mr. Baughman, Urban Tarwater, Mr. Hutchinson, John Walters, and Mr. Waggonshine.

THE THOMPSON FAMILY BAND, C. 1892. This photograph was taken in front of Willis Thompson Sr.'s home. Pictured, from left to right, are (first row) Meville, Walter, Max, and Sarah; (second row) Fay, Willis, and June. The band was in demand for dances and other social occasions.

FAMILY OUTING, 1911. A family poses next to the train tracks with their car. The unidentified driver is wearing a duster to protect his clothing. He looks like he is impatient about waiting for the photograph to be taken, as it seems he wants to get back into the car and drive away.

HARVEY SYKES WITH A THOR MOTORIZED BICYCLE. Hale's childhood label reads, "My papa." Sykes worked on railroad construction for many years and then later owned orange and walnut groves in Orange County.

WASHINGTON AVENUE, 1916. Signs of progress cropped up everywhere, just 35 years after the railroad arrived in the valley. Washington Avenue was the first street paved in Murrieta. The men poured concrete from an early cement mixer, smoothing and packing it to make a 16-foot-wide roadbed. This was the old Highway 395 and 71 that connected Riverside to San Diego.

YOUNG MUSICIANS, 1914. Young people entertained themselves with music and games in an era before electronic entertainment. Pictured here, from left to right, are Hale Sykes at the piano, Willis Maydole playing the mandolin, and George Hale strumming the guitar in the parlor of the Fountain House Hotel.

PEACE PARADE, NOVEMBER 11, 1918. Hale and her friend Putsy Rimmer were so excited about the end of "The Great War" that they paraded down the street to celebrate. Hale displayed the newspaper headline "Germany Surrenders" and Putsy banged on a Chinese gong from the Fountain House Hotel. One of the local farmers chided Hale for upsetting his horse with the noise from the gong. Hale's son Marvin proudly displays the gong in his Murrieta home today.

KATIE SLEEPER AND HALE SYKES, 1907. Hale fed chicken, ducks, and geese under her Aunt Katie's watchful eye in the yard behind the Fountain House Hotel. This was a typical scene outside a kitchen door during this era. Notice the woodpile and the water faucet.

WILLIAM BROWN AND CHILNESSA PARKER AT UPPER RANCH. Brown, an Englishman, ran a dairy with Albert Hutchinson south of town near Brown Street and Adams Avenue. The Hutchinson and Brown Dairy shipped dairy products by train to other areas. Brown Street was named for him.

MR. HIND WITH JOE THOMPSON'S HORSE. The Murrieta hills provided a background to Mr. Hind as he showed the well-groomed horse of Joe Thompson on a clear December day. Hind owned 160 acres on Los Alamos Road where he cleared brush from his land and kept bees and raised grain. The house and land are still owned by the family.

HARVESTING CAMP, 1899. The threshing crew enjoyed the portable comforts of a home camp. The wagon, loaded with bales of hay, testified to a day of hard work. The tent provided shelter from the heat of the day and a secure sleeping place at night. At the end of a long day, workers looked forward to a hot meal from the chuck shack and a cool drink from the water bucket shaded from the sun.

DOG BEGGING MEAT DELIVERYMAN. The Murrieta Meat Market wagon, eventually replaced by a Model T Ford, carried a large assortment of meats and sausages. An undated newspaper ad stated the market sent their wagon to the Elsinore vicinity on Tuesdays and Fridays of each week and said that mining camps could leave their orders for meat at any store.

MEN ON HORSEBACK, 1914. Pictured from left to right, are Arlie Miller, two unidentified men, Mateas Carillo, and Lawrence Miller.

ALICE AND FRED SOTELLO, C. 1931. Two of Eulogio and Jessie Sotello's four children pose at the family home. The family went to the mission in Pala for Catholic services before Saint Catherine's Catholic Church was built in Temecula in 1917. (Photograph courtesy of the Sotello family.)

WINTERS'S DRIVEWAY. The driveway led to the house partially seen to the right of the trees. There were pear trees on both sides of the lane, and they had a large grape vineyard. It was located where Murrieta Elementary School is today. Hale Curran earned her first 10¢ picking grapes there for Joe Thompson.

LOVERS LANE POSTCARD, MAY 5, 1917.
No one remembers why B Street was called
Lovers Lane between Washington and
Adams Avenues. This was where the Fourth
of July picnics were held as depicted on the
book cover.

**LOVERS LANE AFTER
SEVEN INCHES OF
SNOW, DECEMBER 31,
1915.** This is B Street
between Washington
and Adams Avenues
after a rare storm
dumped more than
seven inches of snow.

Rates

Tent Cottages . . . . $10.00 per week (for one person)
Cottage Row . . . . 11.00 & $12.00 per week (for one person)
Old Hotel . . . . 12.00 & 14.00 per week (for one person)
New Hotel . . . . 15.00 & 16.00 per week (for one person)
Tent Cottages . . . . 20.00 per week (for two persons in one room)
Cottage Row . . . . 20.00 & $22.00 per week (for two persons in one room)
Old Hotel . . . . 22.00 & 24.00 per week (for two persons in one room)
New Hotel . . . . 26.00 & 28.00 per week (for two persons in one room)
Rates by day, $1.75 to $2.50 for one person; $3.50 to $4.50 for two persons
Rates for children according to age.

These rates include board, room and baths, with ordinary attention.
Extra charge for special attention.
Free Garage.

Time Table

Two trains leave Santa Fe Station daily except Sunday. Only one train leaves on Sunday.
8:30 A. M. every day, including Sundays.
2 P. M. daily, excepting Sundays.
Free carrying auto bus meets guests for Murrieta Hot Springs at Murrieta Station.
For best auto route inquire of Automobile Club of Southern California — 1344 So. Figueroa Street. Phones: Main 4406; Home 60259.

GUENTHERS' MURRIETA HOT SPRINGS RATES AND TIME TABLE, C. 1914. During this era, the highest daily rate charged by owner Fritz Guenther was $4.50 a day per couple. This included room, board, baths in the hot springs, garage parking, and "ordinary attention." Those guests requiring "extra attention" from the staff were charged accordingly. The American plan included three meals, one mineral bath, and daily use of the swimming pool.

ARRIVAL OF GUESTS AT GUENTHERS' MURRIETA HOT SPRINGS RESORT, C. 1914. A brochure announced the great Murrieta Mud Springs were three and a half miles from the Murrieta Station on the Santa Fe Railroad, and the noted Lincoln Highway passed through the property. A free autobus for guests and baggage met rail passengers and took them directly to the resort over a picturesque road where they felt the touch of sincere hospitality for which the hotel was noted.

GUENTHER'S DAIRY STOCK, C. 1914. The resort, situated where Juan Murrieta once washed his sheep, prided itself on its fresh butter, pure milk, and fresh eggs. An early advertisement boasts, "The meats are excellent, being home productions."

GARAGE AT RESORT, C. 1914. The spacious garage offered "free storage" of automobiles for guests. In early years, before many roads, maps indicated directions like "turn at the windmill," etc. The poor roads and poor reliability of vehicles required the attention from a garage after a road trip.

GUENTHERS'
MURRIETA
Mineral Hot Springs

DINNER
Nov. 23, 1935

Hearts of Lettuce, French Dressing

Cream of Corn au Crouton

25¢ Extra Charge For Steak or Lamb Chops
When Not on Menu

ENTREES
(Choice of One Order Only)

Grilled Salmon, Parsley Butter

Half Fried Spring Chicken on Toast

New York Cut Steak, Maitre d' Hotel

Roast Leg of Pork, Apple Sauce

Hot or Cold Vegetable Plate

Cold Roast Prime Ribs, Potato Salad

Rissole Potatoes, String Beans

Orange Cake, California Apricots
Peach Sherbet
Coffee, Tea, Milk or Buttermilk

Ask Your Waiter For The Wine List

California's Greatest Health Resort

DINNER MENU, NOVEMBER 23, 1935. There was no shortage of elegant food at the resort to appeal to the most discriminating taste. This menu, now a precious memento of the resort, was scratch paper for Hale Curran during the time she worked as a maid at the resort. On the backside of the menu she wrote a shopping list for fabric.

BARBER SHOP, C. 1914. In later years, barber George Hale moved his barbershop from B Street in Murrieta next to the bar at Guenthers' Murrieta Hot Springs Resort. Old-timers remembered that midday was the best time to get a haircut. If they went too early, George was not steady, and by late afternoon, he had made too many trips to the back room for a nip. Ole Larson took over the barbershop after George moved his business to Main Street in Elsinore in the 1950s.

TENNIS COURT AND CROQUET GROUNDS, C. 1914. The resort offered frequent "musical entertainments of high order" and dances three times a week. A brochure states, "A beautiful lawn tennis court, croquet grounds, acrobatic bars, dumb-bells, boxing gloves and punching bags for out-door sport, are all kept in good order. In fact, there are so many things to amuse that it would be impossible to enumerate them."

BILLIARD HALL, C. 1914. Besides advertising the resort as a place for rest and quiet, it also was known for its recreation. "Don't think that things are wanting in the amusement line, for there is almost everything imaginable to please." It is interesting to note from the photograph that women were allowed to play pool in the billiard hall.

PAINTED ROCKS, C. 1904. A brochure states that "mysterious hieroglyphics" were painted on the rocks by "some ancient tribe of Indians." It also mentions that numerous mortars and pestles for grinding were found near the many hot mineral springs of the region. The painted rocks pictured here were destroyed by a developer in 1932. A modern carved rock, a monument honoring Fritz Guenther, is located in Pond Park on Murrieta Hot Springs Road.

TILED POOL, C. 1950. The Great Plunge, the first pool constructed, was situated where the pool is now but was enclosed in a building. In 1929, the pool was renovated and the building removed to allow poolside sunbathing. The resort advertised, "At Murrieta all of Nature's remedies are present, together with the healing waters of the springs."

94

DINING ROOM, C. 1904.
Dining was done with elegance
and good taste. There were
seatings for early dinners at
6:00 p.m. and late dinners
at 7:00 p.m. Breakfasts were
served freestyle. Resort guests
sat at assigned tables and were
served by the same busboy and
waiter for their entire stay. Tips
were collected at the last meal
of the guest's stay.

CHRISTMAS DINNER

DECEMBER 25, 1948

Assorted Nut Meats

Hearts of Celery   Green Onions   Ripe Olives   Radishes

Lobster Cocktail

Salad

California Fruit Salad with Whipped Cream

Soup

Bisque of Oysters

Fish

Halibut Steak, Montpelier Butter

Entrees

ROAST PRIME TOM TURKEY, OYSTER DRESSING, CRANBERRY SAUCE

ROAST LEG OF PORK WITH DRESSING, CANDIED APPLE RING

GRILLED NEW YORK STEAK, SAUTE MUSHROOMS

COLD BAKED HAM, POTATO SALAD GARNIE

CALIFORNIA FRUIT PLATE WITH COTTAGE CHEESE

Vegetables

Creamed Whipped Potatoes   Garden Peas

Candied Yams   French Green Beans

Desserts

Hot Mince Pie   Pumpkin Pie   Fruit Cake

Fruits

Oranges   Apples

Drinks

Coffee   Tea   Milk   Buttermilk

Parker House Rolls

**CHRISTMAS DINNER MENU,
1948.** The menu shows exotic
additions of lobster cocktail
and bisque of oysters to the
traditional Christmas dinner.

KITCHEN AND DINING ROOM STAFF. Headwaiter Max Stone and manager Bud Guenther, whose grandfather Fritz was founder and proprietor of the resort, pose with the staff in this photograph. Waiters wore white shirts and bow ties. Nearly everyone in the Murrieta area worked at the resort in some capacity at one time or another.

Six

SCHOOLS AND LANDMARKS

INVITATION TO THE GRAND BALL, 1885. The event at the new Murrieta schoolhouse celebrated the completion of the school. The organizers included Juan Murrieta, Jose Gonzalez, F. M. Sumner, and other notables. Banker George Fox was on the music committee. What a bargain the event was for $2 per couple, including supper at the Murrieta Hotel.

A Sunday Ride, 1893. With the elementary school in the background, Mr. And Mrs. Bradford rode in a buggy next to the railroad track near the Murrieta Depot. Although the horse is standing still, Mrs. Bradford held the frame just in case of a sudden lurch. The couple shared a lap robe for warmth.

Murrieta School, 1888. No one could get the dog out of the way when the photographer snapped this shot at the first Murrieta schoolhouse. Some of the parents stood behind the students to the left and some older boys stood behind on a wagon. The school bell rang for the first time on October 28, 1885.

SCHOOL. In 1887, teachers were paid $187 each month. There were three teachers in 1916. Children walked to school or rode horses. They climbed over the fence on a stile to get into the schoolyard. A small barn and stable sheltered the horses while students were in school.

MURRIETA SCHOOL. The first school in Murrieta was the lean-to at the Hedges place on the corner of Washington Avenue and Ivy Street, and Mrs. Hedges was the first teacher for the 14 students. The community was proud of the new school where many community meetings and socials were held.

SCHOOL. Students were allowed to attend school barefoot—some went that way because their families couldn't afford shoes and others just because they wanted to be barefoot. A few students didn't wear shoes until high school, when it was required, and their feet were tough and calloused. Some said they put sand in their shoes to feel like they were still barefoot.

PITCHER PUMP AT MURRIETA SCHOOL, 1908. Water for the school was originally hand pumped from the well. The water table was 10 to 12 feet in those days and would draw up to 20 feet with no windmill for mechanical pumping or tank needed. Later the school had a tank and a windmill to supply water to the drinking fountains.

MURRIETA STUDENTS, 1914. Students with Miss Lois Kenaley and a teacher identified as "Mrs. E." were from the families of Lasswell, Thorne, Clogston, Thompson, Freeman, Mornose, Lambert, Rimmer, Peters, Sykes, Hale, Rail, Black, Letner, Reva, Parker, Small, and Peters.

MURRIETA'S SECOND SCHOOL. While the new school was being built, classes met in the drugstore on Third Street called Guild Hall. The second school was built at the same location as the first after they outgrew it. Students would race to get to school early so they could ring the school bell to call pupils to their classrooms. The classrooms of the U-shaped building featured maple desks, slate blackboards, and photographs of Presidents Washington and Lincoln.

PROGRAM FOR THE MURRIETA SCHOOL PLAY DAY, MAY 6, 1941. Play Day, an event students looked forward to eagerly each year, was sponsored by the Guenthers, the Murrieta Hot Springs, the historical society, and the machine shop in 1941. Murrieta students invited the neighboring school districts of Wildomar, Alberhill, and Temecula to compete in relay races, 50-yard dashes, and other fun activities.

MURRIETA STUDENTS, 1925. A barefoot boy who has a rip in the knee of his pants holds a placard that reads, "Murrieta Grammar School, Class of 1925." Principal Mrs. Thayer is to the left and teacher Miss Inman-Kane is to the right. The families names represented include Sierra, Hamilton, Wickerd, Thompson, Buck, Small, Matteson, Stiffler, Davis, Thayer, Stoner, Damiano, Sykes, Morton, Pollard, Lloyd, Hochalter, Dunham, Hackenburg, Brown, Roripaugh, Freeman, Lopez, and Dunham. (Photograph courtesy of the Barnett collection.)

CLASSES IN 1948–1949. Third-, fourth-, and fifth-grade students squint against bright sunlight in this photograph taken in front of the second Murrieta School. Loretta Erdel Barnett is fourth from the right in the top row. Some of the family names represented here include Erdel, Harmon, Saminago, Collins, Rasch, Dunham, Contreas, Barth, Blake, Beauchamp, King, Sheld, Kerdroan, Olivera, and Watkins. The teacher was Miss Harmon. (Photograph courtesy of the Barnett collection.)

SECOND SCHOOL. In the 1950s, when the state deemed the school unsafe, construction of a new one began at a different location. The individual who purchased the property where the second school stood allowed it to fall into neglect. After multiple citations for tall weeds on the property, the building burned. The City of Murrieta now owns the hull of the building and the surrounding property. Several individuals are promoting the renovation of the building for a museum and city recreation center.

THIRD MURRIETA SCHOOL. When the new school opened at the corner of Adams Avenue and B Street in September 1958, teachers Barbara Stillwell (the preachers wife), George Contreras, Rose McClure, and teaching principal Gordon Harmon instructed the students. Cora Stollar did the landscaping around the new school.

CORA STOLLAR'S RETIREMENT, JUNE 1959. Cora was honored for her many years working as the custodian of the Murrieta Grammar School with a retirement party patterned after the television program *This is Your Life*. Pictured, from left to right, are Isabela Rail, George Blake, unidentified, Junettie Biazo, Floyd Rail, David Johnson, Cara Lee Rail, Walt Cooper, Gordon Harmon, Cora Stollar, Rita Domagnea, and Phronia Wickerd.

MILLER'S FALLS. The falls in Miller's Canyon was named for Willard Miller, the Murrieta Depot station agent from the 1890s through the 1920s. He and his brother Eugene built a barn on their property along Hayes Avenue at the west end of B Street. They planted the olive trees as a windbreak and lived in the barn until their homes were constructed.

THE B STREET BRIDGE, FEBRUARY 1978. Water nearly overran the B Street Bridge after six inches of rain fell in six hours. During this season of heavy rainfalls, roads in the Tenaja Valley near the Santa Rosa Plateau were impassible for 30 days, isolating families and livestock. The county sheriff's department, the Murrieta Volunteer Fire Department, and U.S. Marines airlifted supplies into the area until the roads were cleared.

MURRIETA CREEK, LOOKING NORTH, 1958. The Temecula Land and Water Company sold lots in Murrieta by boasting about the "splendid climate" and declaring, "The whole country around Murrieta is abundantly supplied with water." Those farmers who moved to sunny Southern California from the Midwest had a little too much of the abundant water during several rainy seasons.

MURRIETA CREEK, LOOKING SOUTH, 1958. Every family depended on their own wells until after the arid summer of 1962 when several went dry. Concerned citizens formed the nonprofit Murrieta Mutual Water Company, sold shares, and pumped water from several deep wells. Today Murrieta receives water from several water agencies, including the Eastern Municipal Water District.

RAFTING ON FLOODED WASHINGTON AVENUE, 1950s. Johnny Dunham, Gilroy Contreras, and Curtis Thompson drifted down Washington Avenue past the machine shop on a raft made from an aluminum tank mold with Prestone cans attached as flotation devices. A dog sat in the safety of the Murrieta Machine Shop truck.

THE END OF THE RAFT RUN, 1950s. Losing the raft near the slaughterhouse in Temecula, Curtis Thompson, Gilroy Contreras, and Johnny Dunham waded out from their one-way raft trip. Marvin Curran drove his pickup down Highway 395 to gather them up. Marvin says the runaway raft probably banged around in the canyon and ended up in Camp Pendleton.

STROLLING DOWN B STREET. Ronald Wickerd, Satch La Valley, and Marlys La Valley walked toward the Burnham's store. Two cars are visible below the dip in the mountains on the grade on Tenaja Road. In 1978, the county approved Clinton Keith Road, the only way to drive to the top of the mountains above Murrieta. Before Clinton Keith Road was constructed, the Tenaja Grade went through the dip to get to the houses past the Tenaja guard station.

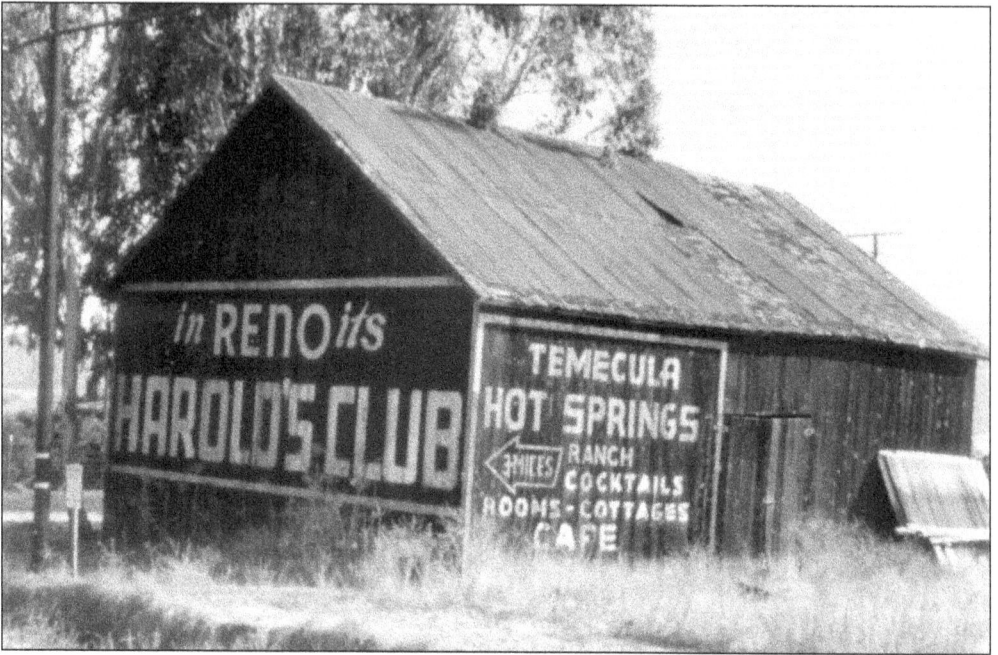

RENO SIGN ON CLIFF THOMPSON'S BARN. Everyone traveling through Murrieta to or from San Diego saw this sign at the corner of Washington Avenue and Ivy Street. This well-known landmark was at the intersection of Highways 71 and 395 at the south end of town, where a number of serious traffic accidents occurred. Charlie Schweitzer owned the property in 1978.

THE OTHER END OF THE BARN, 1976. The barn advertised the Harold's Club in Reno and a little-known Temecula Hot Springs just down the road from the Guenther's Murrieta Hot Springs. The Temecula Hot Springs was never as successful as its neighbor. It changed names with a succession of owners and was called at various times Stillman Hot Springs and Murrieta Springs West.

Leona Cooper Riding Lucky Giles, 1954. Leona promoted youth horsemanship in the Murrieta area. In 1961, she staged a community barbecue and gymkhana. She trained children and teens to study horsemanship and to ride. Leona was a major promoter for building the arena in Murrieta. (Photograph courtesy of the Barnett collection.)

Walt Cooper Riding Lucky Giles, 1954. This photograph was taken beyond Cheney Hills on Old Highway 395 between Murrieta and Wildomar on the old Shaw Place. Walt was a grain farmer. When the rails were removed from the railroad bed in 1935, the oak ties were sold for use in fence posts for 10¢ each. Walt hauled a good many for Murrieta folks. (Photograph is courtesy of the Barnett collection.)

Murrieta Stud Farm Photograph. In the 1970s, Lady Bird Johnson, America's first lady, published a book called *America the Beautiful* with one photograph representing each state. She chose an image similar to this one to represent the state of California. This was taken at the Murrieta Stud Farm owned by B. J. Ritter Ranch.

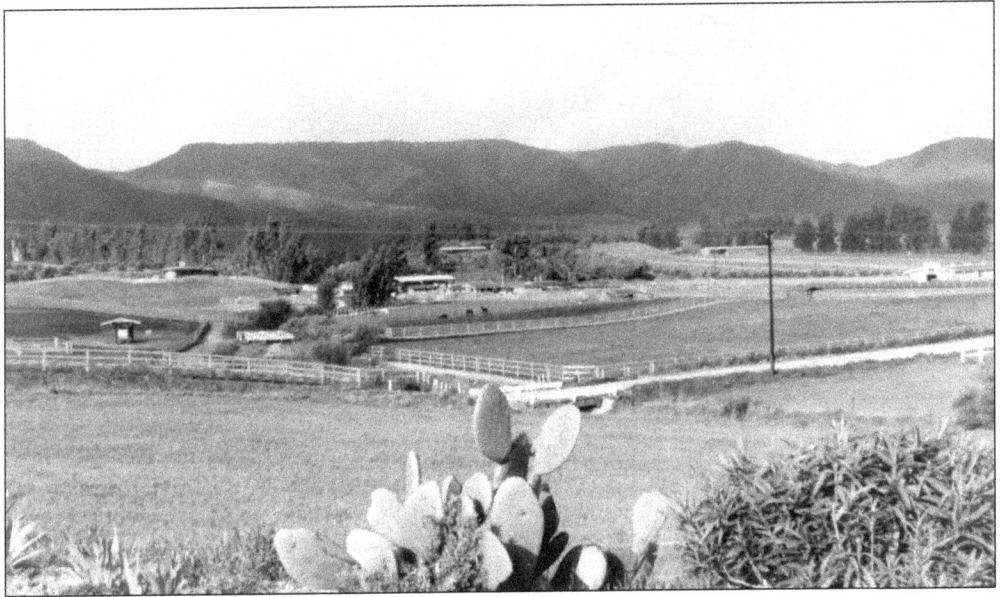

THOROUGHBRED RANCH IN MURRIETA. In the 1960s, people said there were more registered horses than registered voters in Murrieta. There were actually 1,000 registered horses and 1,200 registered voters. Some of the ranches raising Thoroughbred horses included the Murrieta Stud Farm, and the Kidder, Ritter, Shamel, and Pascoe Ranches. One of the ranches had 100 mares that were all in foal at the same time. Workers circulated between the mares to help them give birth to the Thoroughbred foals.

HORSES GRAZING. This ranch near Kalmia Street and Jefferson Avenue was run by a man who had previously owned a Rolls Royce dealership in Beverly Hills. Professional horse breeders loved Murrieta for its clean air and close proximity to the Del Mar and Santa Anita Racetracks, bringing a shift from the traditional dry farming of the community to Thoroughbred breeding and training in the 1960s.

THE WOLF STUMP, DECEMBER 1958. Sons of Raymond and Octavia Thompson, Michael, age 15, and Patrick, age 13, pose by the familiar Murrieta landmark on Washington Avenue sometimes called the Bear's Head. The remnant of a burned-out cedar tree attracted attention, especially after someone painted a white eye and mouth on it. *Ripley's Believe it or Not* featured a photograph of the stump. Larry Humphrey destroyed the landmark when he hit it with his car on April 12, 1964.

Seven

Murrieta
Fire Department

First Murrieta Fireman's Barbecue, 1948. The Murrieta Volunteer Fire Department was formed in 1947 after Max and Mattie Thompson's home burned down. The new department needed firefighting equipment and gear so they decided on a barbecue to bring in the money to purchase what they needed. It was a success—450 people attended the first barbecue. This annual event continues today.

MR. BURNETT AND GIBB MILLER, 1948. The two men rest by the cast iron pot they are cooking beans in for the first annual Firemen's Barbecue. Miller, an old cowboy, taught the firemen how to do deep-pit barbecuing, and he supervised the cooking for the first few years of its existence.

MURRIETA'S FIRST VOLUNTEER FIRE DEPARTMENT, 1948. Pictured here, from left to right, are (first row) Marvin Curran, Lawrence Dunham, Coy Burnett, and Ted Sheld; (second row) assistant chief Vic Garrison, Clayton Erdel, Willis Thompson Jr., Oscar Matteson, Floyd Rail, and Chief Raymond Thompson. The photograph was taken at the dedication of the truck and firehouse.

CHILDREN AT THE FIRST FIREMEN'S BARBECUE, 1948. Preparing to serve, from left to right, are Nelda Sheld, Nadine Erdel, Cora Sheld, Lucy Dunham, Margie Matteson, Winnie Lovett, Octavia Thompson, and Genie Williams; Oscar Matteson is collecting money. Their children and two kids from the Watkins family were anxious to eat. Loretta Erdel Barnett stands sixth from the right in the front row.

THE FIRST FIREHOUSE. The first firehouse was dedicated at the first barbecue. The wood-frame building, like a deep two-car garage with higher doors, was constructed largely from donated materials and labor.

HAULING THE BEAN POT, APRIL 1965. Originally the beans for the Firemen's Barbecue were cooked at the fire station, but in later years, they were prepared at Guenther's Murrieta Hot Springs. When the pots of beans were transported in a pickup truck down the bumpy road to the barbecue site, the lids to the pots bounced on and off and more than a few beans were lost. This photograph shows Betty Jennings and Lucy Dunham handling the pot of beans.

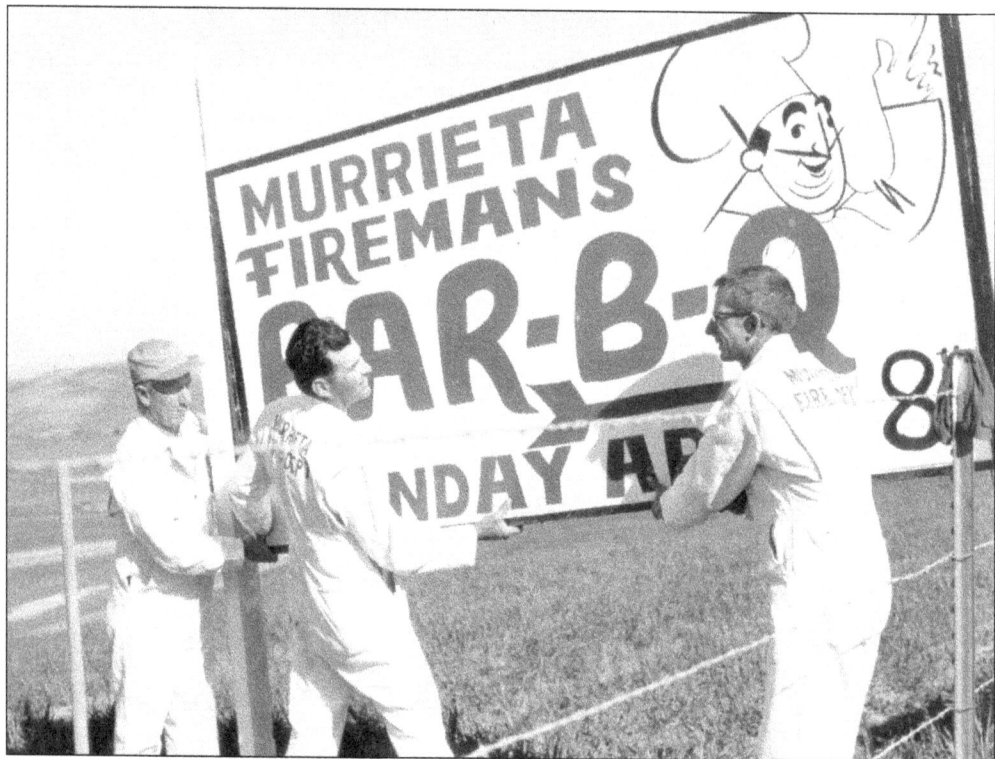

BILLBOARD FOR BARBECUE. From the time of the first firemen's barbecue through the present day, signs are put up in several locations a week before the event. Community support has always been strong for the fire department and the annual barbecue has been the biggest event of the year. Today, since there is funding for the fire department, prices are kept low so everyone can enjoy themselves.

FIREMEN PLANNING BARBECUE, 1962. The men were inside the fire station, wearing their monogrammed coveralls. Pictured, from left to right, are (first row) Ira Rail, Leslie Dunham, Marvin Curran, John Dunham, Ray Thompson, Curtis Thompson, and Mick McGaa; (second row) Bill Jennings, Murrell Jensen, Buck Sheld, and Lawrence Dunham.

FIRST MEAT FROM THE PIT, 1966. Firemen dug the pits by hand with shovels to approximately six feet deep, three feet wide, and five feet long. They started the coals with four to five cords of oak wood at midnight on Friday. By noon on Saturday, the coals were ready for the seasoned boneless square chuck, which was put into white flour sacks and cooked for 24 hours.

4-H BOOTH. After the Firemen's Barbecue became an annual event, several community organizations set up booths to promote their groups and to make some money. This is still being done today. In 2006, Washington Avenue was closed for a street fair called the Block Party from Friday evening through the Sunday of the barbecue.

FIREMEN BY TRUCK, 1949. Pictured here, from left to right, are Willis Thompson Jr., Marvin Curran, Wes Collins, Oscar Matteson, Vic Garrison, Ray Thompson, and Ray Sheckel.

ASSISTANT FIRE CHIEF, 1958. Chief Vic Garrison awarded Marvin the assistant chief's hat and badge when Ray Thompson retired from the position. Marvin became chief in 1974 and served in that capacity until retiring in December 1992.

FIRE IN MOUNTAINS, 1969. The Murrieta Fire Department fought this fire in the mountains that went over the top and burned south almost to Lawrence Welk Village.

QUICK ATTACK UNIT, 1980. This vehicle carried 300 gallons of water to put out a fire under high pressure and was used out in the field.

FIGHTING A GRASS FIRE. The firemen fought fires with these units, the brush truck and quick response unit, with water from high-pressure nozzles. Without hydrants nearby, they carried 300 to 500 gallons of water and conserved it by using 55 gallons a minute at 1,000 pounds of pressure.

BRUSH RIG, 1969. Marvin Curran built this very old but very capable truck. When a volunteer firefighter arrived at the scene of a fire, he was glad to see other volunteers arrive to assist in putting out the blaze.

THE THIRD ENGINE. Fire department volunteers also built this vehicle. Marvin Curran says, "We built all of them. We installed pumps and built tanks, and built up engines. We took a semi-tractor from a car hauler and made a fire truck from it. Funds from property taxes and from the barbecue went to buy uniforms, pay electrical bills, and to build equipment."

SURPLUS OES PUMPER, 1976. The Office of Emergency Services (OES) sold Murrieta's fourth fire engine to the department for $1. This was the first manufactured engine owned by the department.

BUILDING MURRIETA'S SECOND FIRE STATION, 1965. This station, located on Juniper Street across from the town hall, is still in service. It has been added on to and modernized. It is now the headquarters. The town supported a bond to build the station and a contractor instead of volunteers constructed it.

MURRIETA'S FIRST NEW APPARATUS ENGINE, 1986. This was the fifth truck owned by the Murrieta Fire Department. Jim Lattimer, second from the right, chief of the Laguna Beach Fire Department, demonstrated how to use the features of the new truck.

MURRIETA FIRE APPARATUS AND STATION, 1991. Before Murrieta became a city, much of the town's business was conducted at the fire station. By 1991, Murrieta owned multiple engines, three brush trucks, and an aerial platform. While Marvin Curran was chief, his goal was to achieve the highest rating for the fire district, to provide the best service, and to lower the rates for homeowners' insurance policies.

OVERVIEW OF MURRIETA FROM TENAJA GRADE, 1972. The view of open land contrasts with how it looks today under sprawling urban growth. The snake-back road, once the route from Murrieta to the Parker Dear picnics at Rancho Santa Rosa and a cattle road for the Vail Company, was closed to traffic when Clinton Keith Road was built in 1978. Ranch owners have come and gone, and with them many tales of the past have vanished. The authors have attempted to repeat some of the tales heard and to present the stories with Hale Curran's photographs in hopes that the community of Murrieta will always appreciate the people who made it the wonderful community it is today.

Visit us at
arcadiapublishing.com

www.ingramcontent.com/pod-product-compliance
Lightning Source LLC
Chambersburg PA
CBHW050703110426
42813CB00007B/2071